My Summer Vacation Book

Jokes, Puzzles, Games, Activities, Spooky Stories, Silly Songs, and More!

by Stephanie Calmenson
illustrated by Patrick Girouard

Scholastic Inc.
New York   Toronto   London   Auckland   Sydney

"The Pitcher" by Amy Berkowitz is used by permission of the author.

ISBN 0-590-93947-5

Copyright © 1997 by Stephanie Calmenson
Illustrations copyright © 1997 by Scholastic Inc.
All rights reserved. Published by Scholastic Inc.

24 23 22 21 20 19 18 17 16   3/0

Printed in the U.S.A.   40

First Scholastic printing, May 1997

Book design by Laurie Williams

Hip, hip, hooray!
Summer has come.
There's no more school.
It's time to have fun.

Staying at home,
Or going away,
This is the book
You'll need every day.

There are jokes, games, puzzles,
Activities, and more.
Turn the pages
To see what's in store....

This book belongs to

_____
Name

_____
Age

_____
Date

PICTURE PERFECT, TAKE ONE!

This is me at the beginning of the summer.

Draw or paste your picture here.

Gee, I'm good-looking!

SCHOOL'S OUT!

You made it! How was your last day?

My last day of school was:

☐   ☐   ☐   ☐   ☐
terrific   lots of fun   a big relief   no big deal   bad news

I said good-bye to:

Grade:_____

Teachers: _____

Kids: _____

_____

_____

_____

_____

The big event of the day was:_____

_____

_____

_____

VACATION'S IN!

How was your first day?

My first day of vacation was:

☐ ☐ ☐ ☐ ☐
the greatest! okay so-so bor-ing a total bust

Tell all here:

_____ _____

_____

_____

_____

_____

_____

_____

_____

OUT-OF-TOWN VISITS

Summer's a good time for visiting family and friends.
(Maybe.)

These are the people I visited out of town:

_____

Name(s)

_____

Place

_____

Name(s)

_____

Place

_____

Name(s)

_____

Place

This is how I got there:

- [ ] car
- [ ] bus
- [ ] train
- [ ] airplane
- [ ] boat
- [ ] rocket ship
- [ ] horse and buggy
- [ ] mule
- [ ] camel
- [ ] other _____

This is where I stayed:

☐ apartment ☐ trailer

☐ house ☐ tent

☐ motel/hotel ☐ other

I had my own room:

☐ yes ☐ no

I shared a room(s) with: _____

As a guest I was (check one box):

☐ absolutely perfect ☐ mostly well-behaved

☐ okay, so I made a few mistakes ☐ don't even ask

People who visited me and my family:

_____

People who *will* be invited back:

_____

People who *won't* be invited back:

_____

DAY TRIPS

It's new, it's exciting, it's extraordinary!
It's a day trip?

Date:_____

Where I went:_____

Who I went with:_____

What I did:_____

I had a ☐ ☐ ☐ time.
      terrific okay terrible

Date:_____

Where I went:_____

Who I went with:_____

What I did:_____

I had a ☐ ☐ ☐ time.
      terrific okay terrible

Date:_____

Where I went:_____

Who I went with:_____

What I did:_____

I had a ☐   ☐   ☐   time.
        terrific   okay   terrible

Date:_____

Where I went:_____

Who I went with:_____

What I did:_____

I had a ☐   ☐   ☐   time.
        terrific   okay   terrible

Date:_____

Where I went:_____

Who I went with:_____

What I did:_____

I had a ☐   ☐   ☐   time.
        terrific   okay   terrible

CAR-RIDE BINGO

Tired of sitting still?
Don't get cranky — get busy!

Here's how to play the game:

What you need:

Bingo cards. (There's one below to get you started.
Make a batch and take them along in the car.)

What you do:

1. Circle a number on your Bingo card as soon as you
   see it on a license plate.
2. When you've circled a whole line of numbers — up
   and down, right to left, or diagonally — call out
   "Bingo!"(Not too loud, or you'll scare the driver!)

6	8	2	3	4
5	4	9	5	8
0	2	6	2	5
9	7	8	1	7
1	4	3	4	0

Here's a variation in case you forget the Bingo cards:

On a piece of paper, write the name of one of the passengers. Circle
any letter of the name that you see on a license plate. The first one
to circle all the letters wins.

YES, NO, MAYBE SO

Stuck in traffic? Lost? Play this game.

The object of the game is to guess the name of a famous person. This game is for two or more players.

How to play:
One player thinks of a famous person.
The other player asks questions which are to be answered, "Yes," "No," or "Maybe so."

Here are some questions you might start with:
"Is the person living?"
"Is the person male?" or "Is the person female?"
"Is the person a musician?"
"Is the person a writer?"

As you find out the answers, you will be able to ask more specific questions. For example, if the person is a musician, you might ask, "Does the person play the piano?"

And so on...

Variation:
You can decide in advance to use fictional characters instead of people.

FINGERPRINT FRIENDS

Ink Pad + Fingers + Pencils = Pictures!

Here's how to make fingerprint friends:

1. Press any one of your fingers against an ink pad.

2. Roll your inked finger, left side to right, onto an index card or piece of paper.

3. Use the fingerprint to draw your fingerprint friends.

4. Try putting a few friends together to make a cartoon strip.

If you don't have an ink pad handy, use letters or numbers to start your drawings. Here are a few examples:

HAPPY FOURTH OF JULY!

Happy birthday, dear America,
happy birthday to you!

How did you spend the day?
Check off the boxes, fill in the blanks,
solve the picture puzzle, and don't forget
to salute the flag!

How was the weather?

☐　　☐　　☐　　☐　　☐　　☐

cloudy　sunny　rainy　hot　cool　other_____

What did you do?

☐ picnic

☐ barbecue

☐ fireworks

☐ parade

☐ boating

☐ beach

☐ other _____

_____

How old is America this year?_____

Check out the parade. There are ten American flags hidden in the picture. Can you find them?

Check your answers on page 94.

MAIL

PLACES TO GO

From polar bears to Mickey Mouse, there's something for everyone.

Do you know the location of each of these famous tourist attractions? Draw a line from the attraction to its state. Then check off boxes.

I've been there	I'd like to go
☐ ☐ San Diego Zoo
☐ ☐ Empire State Building   Florida
☐ ☐ Disneyworld   Arizona
☐ ☐ Disneyland   California
☐ ☐ Grand Canyon   Texas
☐ ☐ Gateway Arch   Tennessee
☐ ☐ The Alamo   New York
☐ ☐ Statue of Liberty   Missouri
☐ ☐ Graceland

My favorite place:_____

Check your answers on page 94.

You've just arrived at the airport. Your plane is scheduled to take off from Gate 9 in three minutes.
Can you get there in time?

Where is your plane going?_____

Check your answer on page 94.

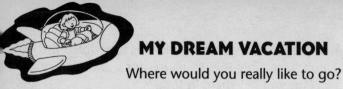

MY DREAM VACATION

Where would you really like to go?

Get a map and pick your spot. Or maybe you've thought up a place that's not on any map at all!

☐ beach
Name the place. _____

_____

☐ cruise
Where would it go? _____

_____

☐ my own back yard
What's your address? _____

_____

☐ mountain trail
Where is it? _____

_____

☐ amusement park
Which one? _____

_____

☐ another state or country
Which one? _____

_____

☐ another planet or galaxy
You name it. _____

_____

☐ other_____

What would you do once you got there?

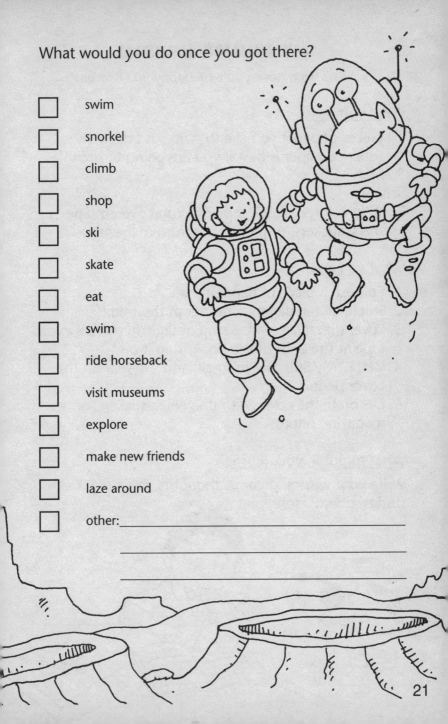

- ☐ swim
- ☐ snorkel
- ☐ climb
- ☐ shop
- ☐ ski
- ☐ skate
- ☐ eat
- ☐ swim
- ☐ ride horseback
- ☐ visit museums
- ☐ explore
- ☐ make new friends
- ☐ laze around
- ☐ other:_____

_____

_____

MY SUMMER JOURNAL

Years from now, you'll be happy you had one.

What you need:

10 pieces of paper you like to write and draw on
    (unlined paper is best if you are going to draw)
Stapler
Scissors
Brightly-colored plastic tape or cloth-covered tape
Markers, stickers, or photos cut from magazines

What you do:

1. Fold each piece of paper in half.
2. Staple all ten papers together at the fold.
3. Cover the staples with a strip of tape. (If there is extra tape at the ends of the book, snip it off.)
4. Write "My Summer Journal" and the year on the cover page.
5. Decorate the cover with drawings, stickers, or magazine photos.

What to put in your journal:

Write your wishes, dreams, thoughts, favorite jokes, stories, poems, songs.

SUMMER TREASURE CHEST

Here's a good place to store the summer treasures that will become your summer memories.

<u>What you need:</u>

A shoe box
Contact paper or foil

<u>What you do:</u>

1. Cover the box with the contact paper or foil.
2. Fill your box with summer treasures: your summer journal, photos, maps, rolled-up place mats, coasters, postcards, rocks, shells, ticket stubs. (If something doesn't fit, make another treasure chest — don't let those memories disappear.)

SUMMER VACATION AT AUNTIE ADDIE'S

Finish this funny story to find out exactly what happened.

Do not read the story first.
On a piece of paper, write the numbers 1 to 19.
Fill in the words or names requested below.
Then read the story using your own words to fill in the blanks.

1. descriptive word   2. descriptive word   3. animal
4. pet's name   5. body part   6. room in the house
7. food   8. vegetable   9. large animal   10. large number
11. man's name   12. number   13. color
14. descriptive word   15. vehicle   16. large number
17. body part (plural)   18. food   19. descriptive word

My ___1___ aunt Addie invited me to spend my summer vacation at her unbelievably ___2___ house.

Her pet ___3___, ___4___, greeted me with a lick on my ___5___.

"Come sit in the ___6___," said Aunt Addie. "I'll give you a big bowl of chopped ___7___, and a tall glass of ___8___ juice."

I was hungry enough to eat a(n) ___9___, so I finished every bite. I was sick for the next ___10___ hours.

When I felt better, Aunt Addie called her neighbor, ___11___, to join us on a picnic. ___11___ was

__12__ feet tall and had ___13___ hair. He was a really

 ___14___ guy. He took us to the park in his old ___15___ .

We had to stop and fix it ___16___ times on the

way.

By the time we got to the park, it was so dark we

could not see our ___17___ in front of us.

So we went back to Aunt Addie's __2__ house

and had a ___18___ supper.

Things got ___19___ -ier and ___19___ -ier after

that. In fact, it was the most ___19___ summer vacation

I ever had.

SUMMER FUNNIES

What's so funny about summer? How about these jokes?

HOT STUFF!

What's black and white and red all over?

A sunburned zebra.

Which letter is the coolest?

Iced T.

Why does a dog get so hot in the summer?

Because he has a coat and pants.

What do frogs like to drink on a hot summer day?
Croak-a-cola.

SILLY STUFF

What do you call a cat at the beach?

Sandy Claws.

What does the sun drink out of?

Sunglasses.

Why did the grizzly bear tiptoe past the campsite?

She didn't want to wake the sleeping bags.

What has two legs, a trunk, and is green?

A seasick traveler.

Why did the chicken row across the lake?

She didn't know how to swim.

ON THE ROAD

What would happen if everyone in the U.S. had a pink car?

We would have a pink car nation (a pink carnation).

Why did the cat refuse to ride in the car?

He was afraid he'd turn into a car pet (a carpet).

How do you get your dog to stop barking in the back seat of your car?

Put him in the front seat.

When can cars drive over water?

When they're crossing a bridge.

When are cars good for swimming?

When they're in a car pool.

IN THE SEA

Which fish are famous?
Starfish.

Are fish smart?
They must be. They travel in schools.

Which fish are rich?
Goldfish.

Which fish do knights like best?
Swordfish.

What do you call a greedy fish?
Shellfish.

Which fish like to harmonize?
Tuna fish.

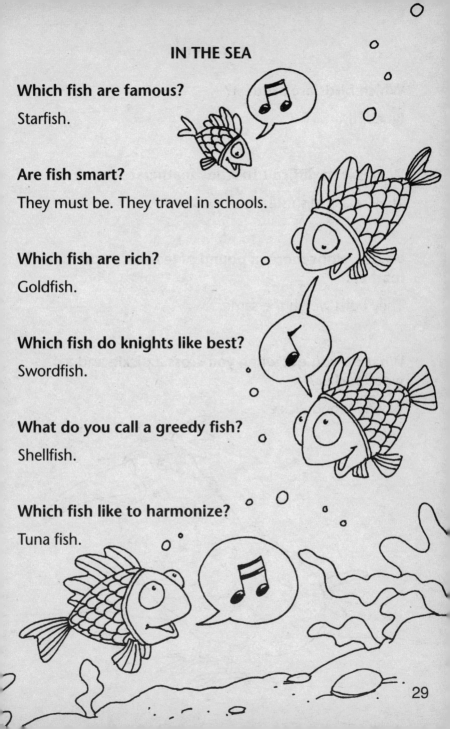

THE BIRDS

Which birds are saddest?

Bluebirds.

Why is it so difficult to study feathers?

They're a ticklish subject.

What weighs more: a pound of lead or a pound of feathers?

They both weigh the same.

What do you get when you cross a pickle and a woodpecker?

Woody Wood Pickle.

THE BEES

Which bees are hard to understand?

Mumble bees.

Which bees hardly ever show off?

Humble bees.

Which bees are acrobats?

Tumble bees.

Which bees do you find in a heap?

Jumble bees.

Which bees make the worst football players?

Fumble bees.

Which bees are looking for a fight?

Rumble bees.

Which bees are clumsy?

Stumble bees.

SUMMER POEMS

Find a quiet place to read a poem,
write a poem, enjoy a poem.

AT THE SEA-SIDE

When I was down beside the sea
A wooden spade they gave to me
   To dig the sandy shore.

My holes were empty like a cup.
In every hole the sea came up,
   Till it could come no more.

Robert Louis Stevenson

POPSICLE POEM

Give it a lick!
Make it quick!
Before it melts
Off the stick.

Plop! It dropped.
That sure is tough.
You didn't lick it
Fast enough.

Stephanie Calmenson

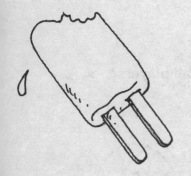

FOURTH OF JULY

I asked my mother for fifty cents
To see the elephant jump the fence
He jumped so high that he touched the sky
And didn't come back till the Fourth of July.

Author unknown

Write your own poem(s) here:

DEAR DIARY

Write about a good day of your vacation.

_____

_____

_____

_____

_____

_____

_____

_____

_____

_____

_____

_____

_____

_____

DEAR DIARY

Write about a bad day of your vacation.

_____

_____

_____

_____

_____

_____

_____

_____

_____

_____

_____

_____

_____

_____

_____

_____

_____

DEAR DIARY

Write about a thing that made you so mad.

_____

_____

_____

_____

_____

_____

_____

_____

_____

_____

_____

_____

_____

_____

_____

DEAR DIARY

Write about a thing that made you so sad.

_____

_____

_____

_____

_____

_____

_____

_____

_____

_____

_____

_____

_____

_____

_____

_____

DEAR DIARY

Write about a funny thing that happened.

_____

_____

_____

_____

_____

_____

_____

_____

_____

_____

_____

_____

_____

_____

_____

DEAR DIARY

Write about an embarrassing moment.

_____

_____

_____

_____

_____

_____

_____

_____

_____

_____

_____

_____

_____

_____

DEAR DIARY

Write about your best summer friend.

_____

_____

_____

_____

_____

_____

_____

_____

_____

_____

_____

_____

_____

DEAR DIARY

Write about your worst summer enemy.

_____

_____

_____

_____

_____

_____

_____

_____

_____

_____

_____

_____

_____

DEAR DIARY

Write about something that made you proud.

_____

_____

_____

_____

_____

_____

_____

_____

_____

_____

_____

_____

_____

KEEP OUT! PRIVATE this means you!

DEAR DIARY

Write a summer secret here.

_____

_____

_____

_____

_____

_____

_____

_____

_____

_____

_____

_____

_____

To keep this page secret, tape a piece of paper over it and write: **PRIVATE**. Use removable tape, so you can read your secret when you want to.

LET'S ROCK!

Are you a rock collector?
Here are some things to do with rocks.

Rock paperweights:

<u>What you need:</u>
A smooth white or light gray rock
Soap and water
Pencil
Tempera paints
Shellac

<u>What you do:</u>
1. Wash the rock with soap and water.
2. Using a pencil, draw a simple picture or design on the rock.
3. Paint the design with tempera paints.
4. When the paints are completely dry, brush the entire rock with a coat of shellac.
5. Let it dry overnight.

Rock sculptures:

What you need:

An assortment of rocks, including several flat ones
Strong glue
Pencil
Tempera paints
Shellac

What you do:

1. Glue rocks together to make animals or people like the ones shown.
2. Using pencil, draw faces and designs.
3. Paint the faces and designs.
4. When the paint is dry, shellac the entire sculpture.
5. Let it dry overnight.

TOP SECRET

Only *you* know the code.

To make your secret code, pick a number from 1 to 5. Add the number you picked to each of the numbers below.

A	B	C	D	E	F	G	H	I	J	K	L	M
1	2	3	4	5	6	7	8	9	10	11	12	13

N	O	P	Q	R	S	T	U	V	W	X	Y	Z
14	15	16	17	18	19	20	21	22	23	24	25	26

Example: If you picked the number 3, then the letter A becomes the number 4 (1 + 3 = 4). B becomes 5. C becomes 6. And so on.

Using this code, what do the numbers 5-8-8 spell? BEE!

Write a summer secret here using your code:

_____

_____

_____

(Keep a record of the number you choose so you can read your own secret!)

GARDENER'S PUZZLE

There are fifteen words from the garden buried in the boxes below. To find them look up, down, forward, backward, and diagonally.

RAKE   HOE   SPADE   WATER   ROSE   SUNSHINE
PEONY   TOMATO   BEANS   LETTUCE   SOIL
MARIGOLD   BUGS   SHOVEL   WEEDS

```
L G B E K A R I M T
E U Y N O E P H O R
V X L I W U G M N Q
O W A H O E A F B E
H A N S O T E S U H
S T W N O Y V D G S
O E C U T T E L S R
K R J S O I L W O O
S P A D E B E A N S
P M A R I G O L D E
```

Check your answers on page 94.

WATER GAMES

It's hot!
Get cool by playing these games.

FIRING SQUAD DODGE BALL

Number of players:
10 or more

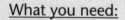

What you need:
One water balloon for every player (balloons should be about 3/4 full when expanded)
A wall to stand against

What you do:
1. Divide players into two equal teams.
2. One team — the target team — stands with their backs to the wall. The other team — the firing squad — stands facing the target team about three feet away.
3. Each player on the firing squad takes a turn throwing a water balloon at a target team player. If the target player catches the balloon, the firing squad player is out of the game. If the target player is hit, that player is out.
4. The team with the last remaining player wins.
5. Begin the game again with the teams switching places.

1, 2, 3, SPLASH!

<u>Number of players:</u>
2 or more

<u>What you need:</u>
One water balloon for each player (balloons should be about 3/4 full when expanded)

<u>What you do:</u>
1. Put balloons close together on the ground.
2. Players make a circle around the balloons.
3. Players count out together, "1, 2, 3!" then run to the center of the circle, grab a balloon, and throw it at any other player while shouting "Splash!"

Try playing this game after a shaving cream (be sure to wear goggles) or whipped cream war. Don't forget to bring your disposable camera — you may never look this messy again.

Paste a
post-game
photo or
self-portrait
here

ICE CUBES

<u>Number of players:</u>
8 or more

<u>What you need:</u>
An ice cube for each team

<u>What you do:</u>
1. Divide the players into two equal teams.
2. At the starting signal, one player from each team picks up an ice cube and tries to melt it without putting it into his or her mouth. Each player keeps the ice cube to the count of ten then passes it on to the next player on the team.
3. The first team to melt its ice cube wins.

THE WATERMELON WATER GAME

Number of players:

2 or more

What you need:

Swimming area
A watermelon

What you do:

1. Mark a goal line at each end of your playing area.
2. Divide players into two teams.
3. Float the watermelon in the center of the playing area.
4. Team members must push the watermelon past the other team's goal line.
5. When finished playing the game, eat the watermelon!

THE HAIRY HAND

It's reaching out to get you....

Did you hear about the kids who wandered into the old haunted house looking for treasure? Here's what happened:

They went into that dark, dark house. It was musty and cold. Every step they took they found themselves caught in another sticky spiderweb.

They climbed a broken stairway to the second floor. They had been told the treasure was buried there. While they were searching they heard a creepy creaking sound. The closet door opened slowly and...

A big, hairy hand popped out! It had six-inch claws that were dripping with blood.

"Ahh!" screamed the kids, as the hairy hand groped toward them.

They ran out of the room and up the steps. The hairy hand was following close behind, reaching out to get them! They ran up one flight, then another. They raced up to the attic. For a moment they thought they were safe. Then one of the kids looked in a mirror hanging on the wall and screamed, "Ahh!"

They could see the hairy hand reflected in the mirror. It was reaching out to get them. There was nowhere to run, nowhere to hide. They all turned their backs and clung the wall, waiting for the hairy hand to decide their fate.

Suddenly, one of the kids felt the hairy hand come down on his shoulder and call out, "Tag, you're it!" (Tap a listener on the shoulder when you say "Tag, you're it!")

UNCLE LOUIE'S WALK

Don't go walking alone!

My Uncle Louie went for a walk late one summer afternoon. He was walking down a lonely dirt path when he met another man walking. The man looked at Uncle Louie and Uncle Louie looked at the man. The man was scared of Uncle Louie and Uncle Louie was scared of that man.

But they kept on walking. It grew dark. The man looked at Uncle Louie and Uncle Louie looked at the man. The man was very scared of Uncle Louie and Uncle Louie was very scared of the man.

But they kept on walking. It grew darker. They came to the woods. The man looked at Uncle Louie and Uncle Louie looked at the man. The man was *really* scared of Uncle Louie and Uncle Louie was *really* scared of that man.

But they kept on walking. It was totally dark and they were deep in the woods. The man looked at Uncle Louie and Uncle Louie looked at the man. The man was *shivery* scared of Uncle Louie and Uncle Louie was *shivery* scared of....

AHHHH!!!

THE PITCHER

Welcome to baseball heaven.

Mike and Bill had been the best of friends ever since they played on the same little league team. Mike was the pitcher and Bill the catcher. They played together all through high school and college, always on the same team.

All through the twenty years that they played baseball together, they both pondered this question: "Is there baseball in heaven?" It wasn't until they played for the Oregon Doves that they made this agreement: Whoever died first would contact the other and report the answer. As it happened, Bill died first. It was a peaceful death at the age of 78, so Mike was not terribly upset. In fact, he was wildly eager to find the answer to his ever-pondered question.

On a Wednesday evening, two days after his death, Bill contacted Mike.

"Mike," Bill said, "I have good news and bad news. The good news is that there is baseball in heaven."

"Then what's the bad news?" asked Mike.

"The bad news? Oh, yes. The bad news is that you're scheduled to pitch tomorrow."

—*retold by Amy Berkowitz, age 12*

NEVER-ENDING STORIES

Try them and see.

PETE AND REPEAT

First speaker: Pete and Repeat were walking down the street. Suddenly Pete disappeared. Who was left?

Second speaker: Repeat.

First speaker: Pete and Repeat were walking down the street. Suddenly Pete disappeared. Who was left?

Second speaker: I said, Repeat.

First speaker: Pete and Repeat were walking down the street. Suddenly…

And so on.

LEFT, RIGHT, LEFT!

Say this one while you're walking. Be sure to be on your left foot when you say, "left," and your right foot when you say "right."

Left, right! Left, right!

Left! Left! I left my guide with forty-eight hikers.

Right! Right! Right in the middle of the camping grounds.

I left! I left! I left our guide with forty-eight hikers.

Right! Right! Right in the middle of the camping grounds.

I left! I left!...

And so on.

WHO DO?

First speaker: You remind me of a man.

Second speaker: What man?

First speaker: The man with the power.

Second speaker: What power?

First speaker: Hoodoo.

Second speaker: Hoodoo?

First speaker: You do.

Second speaker: Do what?

First speaker: You remind me of a man.

Second speaker: What man?

And so on.

THERE WAS A WOMAN AND SHE GOT MAD

Here's a variation on an old favorite song.
Have you ever been this mad?

There was a woman and she got mad.
She jumped into a shopping bag.
The shopping bag did not hide her.
She jumped into a jug of cider.
The jug of cider was too thick.
She jumped onto a walking stick.
The walking stick it broke with a crack.
She jumped onto a horse's back.
The horse got spooked and off he ran.
She jumped into a frying pan.
The frying pan was way too narrow.
She jumped into a big wheelbarrow.
The big wheelbarrow got so rotten.
She jumped into a sack of cotton.
The sack of cotton was terribly tight.
She jumped into some dynamite.
The dynamite blew way up high,
And sent her flying to the sky!

Can you make up some funny verses of your own?

There was a woman and she got mad. She jumped in - to a shop - ing bag

THE BEAR SONG

Here's a long, long song
to sing with friends.

One person is the leader. The leader sings a line and the other singers repeat it. Do this for the first four lines of each verse, then everyone sings the last two lines together.

The other day (the other day)
I met a bear (I met a bear)
A great big bear (a great big bear)
Away out there (away out there)
The other day I met a bear
A great big bear, away out there.

He looked at me (he looked at me)
I looked at him (I looked at him)
He sized up me (he sized up me)
I sized up him (I sized up him)
He looked at me, I looked at him.
He sized up me, I sized up him.

And then he said (and then he said)
"Why don't you run? (why don't you run)
I see you ain't (I see you ain't)
Got any gun!" (got any gun)
And then he said, "Why don't you run?
I see you ain't got any gun!"

And so I ran (and so I ran)
Away from there (away from there)
But right behind (but right behind)
Me was that bear (me was that bear)
And so I ran away from there
But right behind me was that bear.

In front of me (in front of me)
There was a tree (there was a tree)
A great big tree (a great big tree)
Oh, Lordy me! (oh, Lordy me)
In front of me there was a tree,
A great big tree, oh, Lordy me!

The nearest branch (the nearest branch)
Was ten feet up (was ten feet up)
I had to jump (I had to jump)
And trust my luck (and trust my luck)
The nearest branch was ten feet up
I had to jump and trust my luck.

And so I jumped (and so I jumped)
Into the air (into the air)
I missed that branch (I missed that branch)
Away up there (away up there)
And so I jumped into the air
I missed that branch away up there

Now don't you fret (now don't you fret)
And don't you frown (and don't you frown)
I caught that branch (I caught that branch)
On the way back down (on the way back down)
Now don't you fret and don't you frown
I caught that branch on the way back down.

NO GUNS, PLEASE.

IT'S AN OLD SONG. THEY DIDN'T KNOW ANY BETTER!

AND WE'LL ALLOW IT IN A SONG BUT "AIN'T" IS A NO-NO.

THANK YO
PROFESSO

That's all there is (that's all there is)
There ain't no more (there ain't no more)
Until I meet (until I meet)
That bear once more (that bear once more)
That's all there is, there ain't no more
Until I meet that bear once more.

The end, the end (the end, the end)
The end, the end (the end, the end)
The end, the end (the end, the end)
The end, the end (the end, the end)
The end, the end, the end, the end
This time it really is the end!

The oth - er day (the oth - er day) I saw a
bear (I saw a bear), A great big bear (a great big bear), a-way up
there (a-way up there), The oth - er day I saw a
bear. a great big bear a - way up there

DEAR FRIENDS

Are you lazy when it comes to writing letters?
Help has arrived! Just fill in the blanks.

(Here is your basic "Yes, I am still living" letter:)

Dear _____ ,

Hi, how's by you?

Yes, I'm still living. Write back soon.

_____

(You only need to add two names to this letter. So no excuses, please!)

Hi, _____ ,

Heard any good jokes lately? How about these?

Knock, knock.
Who's there?
Letter.
Letter who?
Letter in or she won't stop knocking!

Knock, knock.
Who's there.
Summer.
Summer who?
Summer not very good at writing letters, are they?

Be sure to write back as soon as you stop laughing.

Dear_____ ,

How are you? I am having a _____ time.

The weather has been mostly _____.

I am eating well these days. Last night I had

_____ , _____ , and

_____ for dessert. I have done a few

nice things, such as _____

_____.

I'd like to write more but a big, scary _____

_____ is at my window and I have just enough

time to sign my name before it gets me!

_____

SPORTS FAN'S PUZZLE

There's something for everyone here.

Look up, down, forward, backward, and diagonally for the sports words listed below:

BASEBALL   BASKETBALL   POLO   SWIMMING
TENNIS   FISHING   GOLF   SAILING   SOCCER
RUNNING   BIKING   SQUASH   ARCHERY   JUDO
BOXING

B	N	B	Q	S	I	N	N	E	T
P	A	A	B	I	K	I	N	G	L
J	R	S	W	I	M	M	I	N	G
G	C	K	E	O	H	G	X	I	O
N	H	E	R	B	S	N	H	N	L
I	E	T	E	O	A	I	Z	N	F
H	R	B	C	X	U	L	O	U	O
S	Y	A	C	I	Q	I	L	R	D
I	P	L	O	N	S	A	O	L	U
F	C	L	S	G	E	S	P	K	J

Check your answers on page 94.

GONE FISHING

Has this ever happened to you?

Sara, Debbie, and Nick have their fishing lines crossed.
Which fishing line belongs to which person?
Who caught the fish?

Check your answer on page 95.

RHYME TIME

This summer puzzle is written in rhyme.
Read each clue carefully. Take your time.

ACROSS

1. With rod in hand, make three wishes that you will catch a bucket of _____.

5. Look up and see a pretty sight. With string and a tail, it's a diamond-shaped ____.

6. When you see fireworks in the sky, it's likely to be the Fourth of ____.

8. Beneath the earth grows the potato. Upon a vine, grows the _____.

9. School is out. It's time for fun. Play outside in the summer ___.

DOWN

2. You scream, I scream, we all scream for ___ _____.

3. A nice cold Popsicle is the perfect treat when you are trying to beat the ____.

4. Walk on the beach with pail in hand. Look for sea shells in the ____.

7. When you're sitting by the ocean, put on lots of sun-tan _____.

Check your answers on page 95.

SUMMER MOVIES AND VIDEOS

Which were hits? Which were bombs?
You be the critic!

Write the name of the movie below. Then check off the ratings column. No stars=total bomb. 1 star=okay. 2 stars=good. 3 stars=very good. 4 stars=the best.

What kind of movies do you like best?
Check off the boxes:

horror   comedy   adventure   science fiction   animated

MOVIE MAZE

Quiet please. The lights are out and the movie's about to begin. Can you find your way to your seat without stepping on anyone's toes?

Check your answers on page 95.

SUMMER BOOKS

School's out, so you can read whatever pleases you.

Write the title, the author, and something you want to remember about each book.

1. _____

_____

2. _____

_____

_____

3. _____

_____

4. _____

_____

5. _____

_____

6. _____

_____

SUMMER SONGS

Certain songs are played over and over on the radio
all summer long.

List the songs, and the singers, then check off the
ratings boxes below.

1. _____

☐   ☐   ☐
cool!   so-so   boo-hiss

2. _____

☐   ☐   ☐
cool!   so-so   boo-hiss

3. _____

☐   ☐   ☐
cool!   so-so   boo-hiss

4. _____

☐   ☐   ☐
cool!   so-so   boo-hiss

5. _____

☐   ☐   ☐
cool!   so-so   boo-hiss

6. _____

☐   ☐   ☐
cool!   so-so   boo-hiss

SUMMER READING LIST

Here are books you'll never read.

The Barbecue Cookbook by Lotta Bergers

Your Summer Weather Almanac by Sonny Daize

The Traveler's Atlas by Ware M. Aye

The Summer Moviegoer's Guide by Wayton Lyne

The Beachcomber's Handbook by C. Shelz

Great Railway Vacations by N. Jeneer

Summer Pest Control by Swatte M. Harde

SUMMERTIME TUNES

Here are songs you'll never hear.

Cruise Blues
by Misty Bote

Catfish Blues
by Onda Hook

Snapshot Blues
by Gino Philm

Summer Picnic
by Cole Slaw and Conan D. Cobb

It's My Party!
by Barbie Q.

Splish! Splash!
by N. D. Poole

CREATURE FEATURE

They fly. They crawl. They buzz. They bite.
They're fun to look at.

Look up, down, forward, backward, and diagonally to find the twelve insects listed here:

BEE ANT BUTTERFLY LADYBUG MOTH
GRASSHOPPER SLUG CRICKET FLEA
DRAGONFLY HOUSEFLY FIREFLY

```
D R A G O N F L Y G
S E P J Q P N D S H
F P L B U S L U G B
X P H M E D Y O U U
A O T E J E L C B T
N H O U S E F L Y T
T S M E T J E W D E
I S G K A B R V A R
C A E L F L I N L F
K R S E G O F X H L
A G T E K C I R C Y
```

Check your answers on page 95.

Check off the boxes of the creatures you've seen this summer.

☐ bee

☐ ant

☐ butterfly

☐ ladybug

☐ moth

☐ grasshopper

☐ slug

☐ cricket

☐ flea

☐ dragonfly

☐ housefly

☐ firefly

☐ others _____

_____

_____

_____

SUMMER LUNCH

Tell your friends if they're really nice,
you might invite them over.

Menu

Macaroni salad   Cold cuts/tuna/cheeses   Rolls
Lemonade   Granola fruit bars   Ice pops

MACARONI SALAD

What you need:

Large pot for boiling water
3 quarts water
8 ounces elbow macaroni
1/2 cup mayonnaise
2 tablespoons vinegar (optional)
2 stalks celery, diced
1 teaspoon salt (optional)
1/2 teaspoon pepper (optional)

What you do:

1. Bring water to a rolling boil.
2. Drop macaroni into water and stir.
3. Bring water to a boil again and cook, uncovered,
   for 8 minutes.
4. Drain.
5. Rinse with cold water to cool.
6. Mix in remaining ingredients. You may want to try
   adding other things, too: chopped olives, green
   pepper, scallions. Be daring!

GRANOLA FRUIT BARS

What you need:

Small saucepan
8-inch baking pan
2 tablespoons butter
18-ounce jar fruit preserves
3 cups granola
4 tablespoons confectioner's sugar

What you do:

1. Melt the butter in the saucepan.
2. Add the fruit preserves.
3. Mix and cook over low heat until the mixture is bubbling actively.
4. Remove mixture from heat and let cool.
5. Add the granola and mix well.
6. Grease an 8-inch baking pan and dust with 2 tablespoons of sugar.
7. Pour in the mixture.
8. Dust the top with rest of sugar.
9. Cut into squares (makes about 16).

LEMONADE

What you need:

8 cups of water
12 tablespoons lemon juice (from a bottle or from fresh
        lemons)
1 1/2 cups of sugar
A large pitcher or thermos
A tray of ice cubes

What you do:

Mix water, lemon juice, and sugar together in a large
pitcher or thermos. Chill. Taste, then add more of whatever is needed. Serve in cups filled with ice.

ICE POPS

What you need:

Small paper cups
Fruit juice
Wooden sticks

What you do:

1. Fill each cup about three quarters of the way full.
2. Put the cups in the freezer.
3. After about 45 minutes, check the cups. When ice crystals have begun to form, put a stick into the center of each cup.
4. Put the cups back in the freezer for about three more hours.
5. When the pops are frozen, peel off the paper cups and enjoy.

(QUICK POPS: Instead of waiting for ice crystals to form, put the sticks into the cups when you fill them with juice. The sticks will lean against the side of the cups and the pops will be lopsided, but lopsided pops taste just as good.)

GLUB, GLUB, GLUB!

Don't go swimming alone!

Do not read the story first.
On a piece of paper, write the numbers 1 to 20.
Fill in the words or names requested below.
Then read the story using your own words to fill in the blanks.

1. descriptive weather word 2. item of clothing
3. any object (plural) 4. number 5. large animal
6. body part 7. descriptive word 8. descriptive word
9. body part 10. descriptive word 11. a number
greater than one hundred 12. body part 13. an object
14. an object 15. an object

It was a ___1___ day so I headed for Lake Hi-dee-ho. When I got there, I put on my swimming ___2___ and took a walk along the shore. I found many interesting ___3___ and put them in my bucket.

After my walk, I took a nice ___4___ hour nap. I was awakened when a big, hairy ___5___ kicked sand on my ___6___ .

It was time for a dip in ___7___ Lake Hi-dee-ho. I swam out to the middle where something slimy and ___8___ grabbed my ___9___ and pulled me down!

I struggled with the ___10___ underwater beast. Splish! Splash!

"Glub! Glub!" I called. But no one heard me.

That was ___11___ years ago. So if you're ever swimming in Lake Hi-dee-ho and something touches your ___12___ , it's not a ___13___ , or a ___14___ , or a ___15___ ...

"Glub, glub, glub — boo! It's me!"

IT'S ALIVE!

The answers to this puzzle
are all living things.

ACROSS

2. Look for these mammals flying at dusk, gobbling insects.

3. A kind of shellfish, or a grouchy person.

6. Bzzz. Bzzz. If you bother them enough, they may sting you.

7. First they are tadpoles, then they are _____.

8. These tiny insects may be living on your pet.

DOWN

1. First it's a caterpillar, then a beautiful _____.

2. They have feathers and wings and some sing pretty songs.

4. You may see these insects marching across your picnic blanket, or down, down into the ground.

5. It's small, cute, eats cheese, and will run from a cat.

7. You'll find them underwater, swimming in schools.

Check your answers on page 95.

TONGUE-TRIPPING TWISTERS

Say the title of this page three times fast!
Try doing the same with the twisters below.

Benny's brave bumblebees buzz best.

Seven summer swimmers swim swiftly.

Sally sells seashells by the seashore.

She shall sell her seashells soon.

Twins travel twin trains to Trenton.

We shall see the sun shine soon.

Six sharks in shades sunning.

Write your own twisters here:

_____ .

_____ .

_____ .

_____ .

_____ .

_____ .

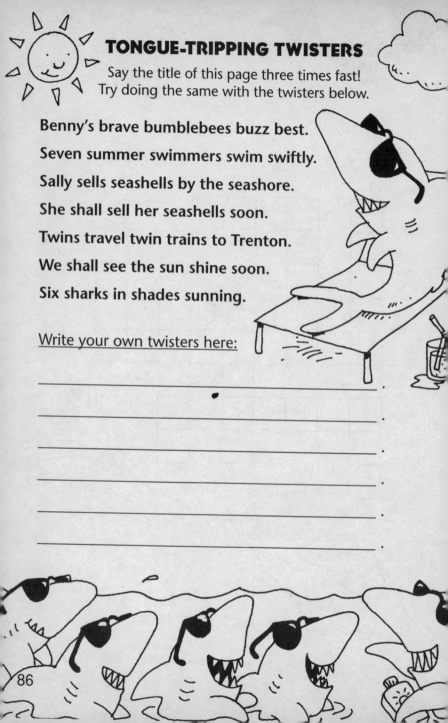

HINK-PINKS

Read these, then make up your own.

A hink-pink is a riddle answered by two one-syllable words that rhyme.

Here are a few:

What do you call sad footwear?
Blue shoe.

What do you call a song sung only at night?
Moon tune.

What do you call a guppy's dream?
Fish wish.

A hinky-pinky is a riddle answered by two two-syllable rhyming words:

What do you call comical rabbit?
Funny bunny.

What do you call a talkative taxi driver?
Gabby cabby.

What do you call waves in the Atlantic?
Ocean motion.

WHAT I DID THIS SUMMER

How many times can you say,
"Been there. Done that."

Check off all the things you've done and tell a little about them:

☐ day camp _____

☐ sleepaway camp _____

☐ water sports _____

☐ video games _____

☐ street games _____

☐ amusement parks _____

☐ hosted friends or family _____

☐ visited friends or family _____

☐ went to the beach _____

☐ went to a lake _____

☐ learned a new sport, game, etc. _____

_____

☐ watched TV _____

☐ read _____

☐ listened to or played music _____

_____

☐ gardening _____

☐ sewing _____

☐ cooking _____

☐ horseback riding _____

☐ bike riding _____

☐ skating _____

☐ daydreaming _____

☐ bird or bug watching _____

Write in other things you did below:

_____

_____

_____

_____

VACATION REPORT CARD

What kind of summer was it?

Check off the box that best describes your summer:

Overall, my summer was:

- ☐ terrific!
- ☐ great
- ☐ good
- ☐ okay

- ☐ Could have been better
- ☐ Not so hot (except for the weather)
- ☐ Bummer summer (boo-hiss!)

Most of the time the weather was:

- ☐ perfect
- ☐ too hot
- ☐ too cool
- ☐ rain, rain, and more rain (get the idea?)

Activities:

- ☐ Lots of fun
- ☐ Good enough
- ☐ Boring (yawn)

- ☐ Thank goodness school's starting (Now that's bad)

Write the things you would do differently next summer:

First of all, I would _____

_____

Secondly, _____

_____

I definitely would not _____

_____

And as for _____

_____ , no way!

YOURS TILL ...

Saying good-bye at the end of summer can be sad.
You'll need some funny farewells.

Yours till the ocean waves.

Yours till the board walks.

Yours till ice screams.

Yours till Bear Mountain gets dressed.

Yours till sandwiches ride broomsticks.

Make up your own here:

_____

_____

_____

_____

_____

KEEP IN TOUCH

Did you make new friends this summer?
Write their addresses here so you can keep in touch.

Name: _____

Address: _____

_____

Phone Number: _____

Name: _____

Address: _____

_____

Phone Number: _____

Name: _____

Address: _____

_____

Phone Number: _____

Name: _____

Address: _____

_____

Phone Number: _____

PUZZLE SOLUTIONS

HAPPY FOURTH OF JULY, p. 16-17

PLACES TO GO, p.19

San Diego Zoo

Empire State Building

Disneyworld

Disneyland

Grand Canyon

Gateway Arch

The Alamo

Statue of Liberty

Graceland

Florida

Arizona

California

Texas

Tennessee

New York

Missouri

PLACES TO GO, p.18

GARDENER'S PUZZLE, p.47

SPORTS FAN'S
PUZZLE, p.66

PUZZLE SOLUTIONS

GONE FISHING, p.67

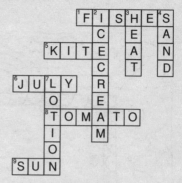

RHYME TIME, p.69

MOVIE MAZE, p.71

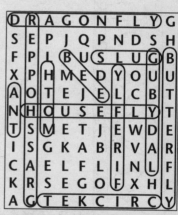

CREATURE FEATURE,
p.76

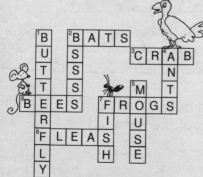

IT'S ALIVE, p.85

PICTURE PERFECT, TAKE TWO!

This is me at the end of the summer.

Draw or paste your picture here.

Wow! I look even better than I did
at the beginning of the summer!